Dog Love
& Dog Loss

Other books by Camille Pavy Claibourne

Pathways to Hope

Dying in God's Hands

Purses & Shoes For Sale:
The joys and challenges of caring for elderly parents

Dog Love
& Dog Loss

CAMILLE PAVY CLAIBOURNE, APRN, PhD

Acadian House
PUBLISHING
Lafayette, Louisiana

On the Cover – *AJ (the Golden Retriever) and Heidi (the German Shepherd) watch with keen interest as their owners (the author and her husband) eat dinner. Could there be a few bits of meat for polite dogs that keep their distance from the table?*

The Acadian House Publishing Speaker's Bureau can bring authors to your live event. For more information or to book an author, contact Acadian House Publishing at (337) 235-8851, Ext. 104, or info@acadianhouse.com.

Library of Congress Control Number: 2021950496

ISBN-10: 1-7352641-9-9
ISBN-13: 978-1-7352641-9-6

• Published by Acadian House Publishing, Lafayette, Louisiana (Edited by Madison Louviere; Trent Angers, co-editor; pre-press production by Allison Nassans)
• Printed by Royal Palm Press, Punta Gorda, Florida

Preface

God created man and animals to co-exist on this beautiful earth and that relationship has provided me with lessons I would not have learned otherwise.

This book is about four decades of adventures of living with and caring for five dogs with my husband, Bill. Early in life, I had various small pets such as hamsters, fish, turtles and even a cat named Wenckebach. Dogs, however, have become part of my soul's journey.

Our dogs have transformed my life, as you will read in the following stories. The experiences that we had together are still vivid in my mind. Some examples are getting locked out of the house naked, returning chewed up shoes to our neighbors, playing the piano with my dog singing along, and enjoying a BBQ with friends while our dog jumped up and stole some of our food.

Four of the dogs featured in this book have died. Their lives were adventurous and their deaths, heartbreaking. Pet loss is not always understood, sometimes not spoken about and often discounted.

As a hospital RN I have worked in many departments. Each unexpected death of a patient stays in my heart and mind while the profound sadness is staggering and chaotic.

Outside of working at the hospital, my nursing journey had no walls as life has called me to help dying friends, family, colleagues, in-laws and parents.

The mysteries in dying and death became my life's calling as I began to learn more about the dying process.

Initially, I was struck by the avoidance and difficulty associated with the topic itself. Why is talking about death and dying so hard? My questions led to a more focused graduate study on death and dying, otherwise known as thanatology. I conducted academic research while interviewing people dying in hospice care. Following graduation I published my work, *Dying in God's Hands*, in 2007.

While in graduate school, my first dog, Pete Moss, died in 1999. The day he died was my introduction to grieving a beloved pet.

I was introduced to a grief workshop for pet owners where I met others who were seeking a private space to talk about the deaths of their pets. They also could not imagine life without their pets and wanted to share the experience of having a pet loss become a journey. It was this group of pet owners who understood that Pete Moss was not just a dog, but family and a beloved friend to all who knew him.

Grief is hard and the journey is not for the faint of heart. However, having support makes the road less painful to travel.

My dogs have been present during difficult life changes such as death, rejection, infertility, illness or hospitalization and surgery. Even when I experienced failure or sadness, our dogs were always happy to see me. When I was tired or lacked energy, our dogs loved me anyway.

Each dog brought a joy to my life that was unique and memorable. When their lives came to an end we lost that unconditional love. I wanted our dogs to live forever.

It was through the loss of our pets, grief and gratitude for having had fun dogs that I was motivated to tell their stories.

Cast of Characters

Pete Moss
(August 1984 – April 1999)

Pete Moss was our first dog as a married couple. He was found in the country, where we lived, in Youngsville. This German Shepherd moved and changed with us from our early days as newlyweds and busy professionals. Pete Moss was adventurous and smart. Together we adapted to city life in Houston, Texas, and then back to urban life in Lafayette, La. Pete Moss made new friends wherever we went. During his 15 years of living large, Pete Moss taught me about accepting change and adventurous living.

Andy
(October 1991 – April 2006)

Andy, our first Golden Retriever, was found by Pete Moss, who brought him home one day. He lived for 15 years during a busy career time for us. He was present during job changes, promotions, deaths, births and house renovations. Andy loved to love and be loved, and was amazing in every aspect. Andy taught me the gift of presence.

Buddy
(October 2000 – July 2012)

Buddy, our second German Shepherd, was the self-proclaimed "dog mayor" of our neighborhood. Buddy supervised the road construction from gravel to pavement. He also watched over house construction, chased cars, was round-up captain for other dogs on the street, and became the number one witness to Bill's retirement years. Buddy taught me about joy and mastering a skill.

A J
(December 2006 – August 2017)

A J, our second Golden Retriever, was adopted as a six-weeks-old puppy. He was a small bundle of fur. His heartbeat matched mine and we instantly became soul mates for life. A J was a witness to my transition from full-time corporate executive to part-time work so I could be one of the primary caregivers for Mom and Dad in their aging and deaths. A J taught me to slow down, love more and smile more.

Heidi 'Enigma' Lou
(January 2014 – Present)

Heidi, our third German Shepherd, was rescued from squalid conditions at six months old. She is our first female dog, and we thought that she would be easier to handle than our male dogs. We were wrong! She is extremely smart, anxious, loyal and beautiful. However, she harbors some strange behaviors which led to her middle name, Enigma. She sticks to us like glue, has a mean, intense bark and uses it plenty! Her antics, facial expressions and odd behaviors communicate intensity. Heidi is teaching both of us patience!

Greetings from Camille, AJ and Buddy.
We hope you enjoy our book!

Table of Contents

Dog Love & Dog Loss

"Dogs come into our lives and teach us about love and loyalty.
They depart to teach us about loss.
A new dog never replaces an old dog;
it merely expands the heart."
– Erica Jong

Chapter 1

A growing fascination with dogs

Our dog journey began with a German Shepherd, Pete Moss, who showed up at our back door. He had been dumped in the ditch on our property. Our second dog, a Golden Retriever that we named Andy, was found in our flower bed visibly beaten and malnourished. Over the years, we purchased two dogs, Buddy and AJ. Our current dog, Heidi, is a rescue.

My fascination with dogs continues to grow by watching and enjoying their varied characteristics and personalities. A dog's beauty is God's creation in action, whether purebred, mutt, large, small, puppy or mature. Our dogs have all been large in size, though my fascination has no boundaries for size or shape.

The colors and unique patterns in their fur tell a story. The wag or position of their tails give distinct signals. The communicative head twists and eyebrow movements are unique forms of expression. Their eyes speak volumes.

I am intrigued by German Shepherds' "radar ears," especially when their eyes are closed. The ear movements are often in sync with our conversations. Out of a dead sleep, they wake to the sound of the refrigerator door or the word "run." And, of course, there is the obvious body language of tail wagging – a good indication of happiness.

Not all body movements are clear. A German Shepherd has ears that are known for auditory vigilance, particularly when guarding property, herds or people. The positioning of German Shepherds' ears can show us their moods. Having the ears up and facing forward means they are attentive, while having the ears pinned back and down could indicate fear, anxiety or guilt. Golden Retriever ears are extra fun when they go up slightly, indicating interest, play time or mischievousness.

Eye contact and voice recognition elicit head tilts, facial expressions and position changes. Our German Shepherd's eyes are like her superpower, not missing a single movement, whereas the Golden Retriever's eyes go straight to the soul.

Then there are irksome characteristics, like waking me in the middle of the night. Maybe the moon is full or there are sounds of an intruding squirrel or possum outside. Incessant barking at the Postal Service truck is annoying as are the sharp puppy teeth that create permanent imprints in furniture. Then, there is the strong, large wagging tail that clears items from the top of the coffee table.

Most of our dogs can tell time by their stomachs. Breakfast and dinner are served in 12-hour increments. Treat time involves a pre-treat time barking for 10 to 15 minutes. If the barking does not move our feet closer to the treat can, they sit close and stare as if to levitate us into action. Sometimes our dogs lie belly up so we can clearly see them to ensure mealtime is not missed.

Our dogs loved stalking a squirrel in the back yard regardless of never having caught one. AJ loved chasing lizards until a lizard started chasing him. Pete Moss and Andy were great at finding rabbit holes and falling asleep before a rabbit ever came out. AJ never missed a water bowl in which to stick his head. And Heidi, just wanting to check in, frequented the pantry door where the food was located.

* * * * *

Over the years, I have learned valuable life lessons about dogs.

• A wet nose at your bedside is better than an alarm clock.

• Large dogs will dig large holes.

• Dogs are more fun to be around than some people.

• If the dog is a digger, he will always be a digger until trained not to be.

• If a dog is courageous, he will become a beacon of courage.

Regardless of how our dogs came into our lives, their traits, quirks, and presence created a sense of love and companionship that can be hard to explain. I now understand what people mean when they say that a dog is man's best friend.

Our dogs' adventures have taught us valuable

lessons and forced us to replace chewed furniture, pillows or carpets. However, they have also introduced us to incredible veterinarians, vet techs, ER vets, pet store employees, neighbors, and other pet owners.

A bundle of warm, furry, and unconditional love always waits for us at the end of the day! Love on a rainy day. Love when we are sick or had a rough day at work. Love when we are tired. Love always.

Chapter 2

Pete Moss
Always the digger
(August 1984 – April 1999)

In 1984, we lived on an acre of land in the country. There was ample space for a large vegetable garden and rose bushes that I could cut to make flower arrangements. We had enough yard to own a riding lawn mower, while a breezeway and covered back porch were great spaces for barbeques on warm afternoons in Louisiana.

We talked about getting a dog. Bill and his family knew a lot about dogs, having had many over the years – ten in all during his childhood. He loved dogs and wanted us to have one as a newly married couple but remained patient with me as I contemplated the idea.

I had never owned a dog. My dad, a pediatrician, trained in the 1940s and had treated cases of rabies in humans. He grew up on a farm with nine siblings and cared for farm animals such as goats, cows and chickens. None were considered pets. Mom also had nine siblings and her family had a few hound dogs, which were cared for by my grandpa.

Knowing that I enjoyed bike riding for exercise,

Bill bought me a bike for my birthday. The next morning, I woke up early anticipating a bike ride before work. When I opened the door, there was a small German Shepherd puppy on the back porch. He had one ear partially up and the other ear completely folded over. His head was cocked to the right as if to say, "Who are you? Where am I? What's the plan today?"

He had mostly black fur with light gold coloring around his face and belly. His legs had enough blond coloring that it seemed he had dipped his paws in light blond paint. His mesmerizing puppy dog eyes had beautiful black markings around them.

Keeping my eyes on him, I yelled, "Bill, did you get me a puppy for my birthday?"

"What?" he yelled back as he was dressing for work.

"Did you get me a dog?"

"What? A dog? No, I got you a bike. What are you talking about?"

"Come see this puppy dog at the back door," I replied.

Coming around the corner and talking directly to the puppy, Bill says, "Well, aren't you a cute one," as he smiled and leaned over to pet him. "You must be lost, and I bet someone is missing you. We should put up 'Found Dog' signs. He looks like a purebred German Shepherd and may be someone's dog. We can ask our neighbors. If no one claims him and you decide to feed him, you will have a dog. He will

Pete Moss

*Pete Moss and his
dear friend, Andy*

claim this house as his own. That's the way it works."

Bill went off to work and I went for my bike ride to think and plan how to make the signs, get copies made at lunch and then post them after work. I got my camera and took a picture of the pup to put on the poster.

Biking down the first block, I heard him running after me. I thought this was good because I could see if any of the neighbors might be looking for their dog. There were not many neighbors out at 6 a.m., but I looked anyway.

I returned home from the bike ride and got ready for work. As I locked the house, the puppy was sitting and staring at me, looking hungry. I got a bowl of milk for him, placed a towel in the garage, and off I went, still recalling what Bill had told me about feeding him.

All day I thought of that puppy. On one hand, I thought of the happy faces of his owners upon finding him, but I also could not help wondering if fate had played a role in this puppy landing, quite literally, on my doorstep. Was God sending me this puppy for reasons I did not yet understand?

Grudgingly, I made the flyers.

The pup was waiting for me when I got home and came with me throughout the neighborhood as I put up "Found Dog" signs. I just knew that someone would claim him, but my heart had already fallen in love.

That evening I called Jane, Bill's mom, to thank

her again for a fun birthday celebration and gifts. I told her about this puppy showing up and before I finished my sentence she said, "If you feed him, he will stay, and you have a dog. That's the way it works."

Week one went by, and no one called about a lost dog. Week two passed and still no calls. I quit worrying about it, named him Pete, and figured he was officially ours! We were excited about having him around.

With my new bicycle, Pete and I exercised together every day with him running at my side. He followed us and anyone who came to visit. He loved being around the yard from sunrise to sunset. He thought he was helping with the yard work as we prepared the flower beds. When we turned our backs, he dug into them. It was a game to him!

He was a digger! There was no question about that. We would work in our yard on weekends off, planting, mowing and making flower beds. We would go to work on Monday only to come home to Pete sitting in one of our flower beds in a man-sized hole he had dug for us. At his side were the dead plants that he had dug up.

With his ears beginning to stay up, he conveyed a proud look, maybe even thinking he did yard work for us. Our beds were often made of mulch, compost and peat moss. With all the digging, his middle name became Moss. After we spread peat moss, he would find a quiet time when we were away to dig it up.

We have many pictures of him with dirt on his nose and peat moss all over his ears while acting like he was innocent.

Pete Moss was the perfect name.

The perfect gift

One February, Bill spent weeks preparing a special rose bed for me as a Valentine's Day gift. The landscape timbers were designed and cut perfectly. There was lattice wood fencing, wood railing on one side, fertilized soil and nine rose bushes at the elevated height with color varieties like an oil painting.

Once completed, it was a picture-perfect flower bed. Bill's dad, Doug, helped to get it all accomplished. A completed flower bed and the end of a busy weekend led to a Sunday afternoon barbeque with the family and many pictures being taken as we admired our new rose garden.

On Monday afternoon, we returned home from work to find Pete Moss sitting in the middle of the rose bed! Five of the nine bushes were dug up with dirt, moss and mulch all around the porch, driveway and walkway. It was a disaster!

Pete Moss was so proud of himself! It had probably taken most of the day to complete the digging. We chased him all around the yard to fuss at him, but he thought it was a game and never got the message. Over the years, he would dig up small trees, gardens, flower beds and plain dirt just for the satisfaction of digging.

Jane, being a dog lover herself and quite an expert, would say, "You can't break a digger."

Having a puppy was fun, though I really did not know much about dog care. Bill and his family, however, taught me many things. I loved having an outside mate to exercise, play fetch, wrestle or just hang out. I wanted him to learn how to fetch our newspaper at the end of our driveway and bring it to us in the morning. He eventually learned how to fetch quite well. Newspaper retrieval, however, was probably not the best thing to teach him. He was so proud of getting a treat when he brought the newspaper to us from the long driveway, but if we did not wake up early to grab the paper from him, it might be chewed up. One Sunday, he brought home all of the neighbors' newspapers! He chewed most of them and we ended up buying and replacing many newspapers that morning.

Pete Moss loved wrestling with a towel, and if he won, he ran the towel around the yard and eventually returned it to the back porch filthy and chewed. I learned to have "dog towels" easily accessible outside.

A certifiable dilemma

One Monday morning that I will never forget, the towel-wrestling trick backfired on me, big time.

The weekend prior was filled with chores and yard work. Living out in the country, with no alarm system and neighbors a few acres away, we felt the need for a little more security, so we purchased deadbolt locks for our doors and installed the locks and secured the windows.

Monday morning was busy, as usual, getting ready for a full week of work. Bill was heading to work first since he had an early meeting. As he headed out the door he yelled and asked me to feed Pete.

Just finishing my shower, I grabbed a towel and headed to the kitchen to get Pete's dog food and bring the dog bowl to the back porch to feed him. Bill was loading up his car for work, and as usual he locked the door and drove off. After feeding Pete and realizing the doors were dead-bolted, I had to think quickly as there was no key hidden outside for me to re-enter.

Do I break the window, or do I try to catch Bill driving away? There was a highway near the back of the property that he would have to travel on after leaving the neighborhood.

Think quickly, Camille, you are naked, and you need to get to work, I thought.

With that in mind, I thought if I ran down to the ditch line, jumped the ditch and flagged Bill down, he could come back and open the door.

Well, Pete thought it was game-time. He grabbed one end of the towel with his teeth to play, leaving one end for me to cover what I could of my body.

I saw Bill's car coming and jumped the ditch in time for him to see me as he was peacefully admiring our freshly mowed yard. He looked up to see me and hit the brakes while laughing and trying not to crash the car. He later said:

"I saw my wife naked and flagging me down with the puppy hanging from the towel trying to play. I thought she was nuts!"

"What the heck are you doing?" Bill asked.

"I'm locked out of the house and need you to come back home to let me in!"

Pete Moss was so happy that we got to run and play before work. The rest of the day, I felt grateful to be fully dressed.

* * * * *

Pete got to spend many of his days with Red, our neighbor's Doberman Pinscher. Pete and Red would run the neighborhood morning and afternoon, visiting, chasing rabbits and barking at various things. They would spend quiet time sitting under a tree together watching the world go by. Nobody messed with a German Shepherd and a Doberman Pinscher.

Most days, Pete Moss was safe at home and stayed out of trouble, until one day he came home bleeding. He had been shot. We discovered several pellet holes and raced him to the vet. We were lucky that none of the pellets hit an organ. The surgery went well to remove most of the pellets. He stayed at the vet's office for a week, and once home again, he recovered well. He did not venture to that area of the highway again.

When disaster strikes

Within a year of finding Pete Moss, our house flooded, along with most houses in our neighborhood. A devastating experience for everyone.

Sam, the neighbor across the street, had a small boat to rescue Bill, Pete Moss and me. We were doubly blessed as Bill's parents, Jane and Doug, lived nearby and opened their home to us and Pete Moss.

They lived in a nice neighborhood and Pete Moss loved going to visit them as their neighborhood had other dogs and many people who walked or jogged. He made friends with anyone who dared to approach a German Shephard unannounced. One day, he ventured off and visited various houses, taking a single shoe and bringing it to the back door at Jane and Doug's.

He brought close to a dozen non-matching shoes to their back door, extremely proud of his "catch of the day." I guess this was his payment for rent while we were flooded out. Doug spent a full day going house to house to match the shoes with the neighbors, apologizing for Pete's rude yet playful behavior. Thankfully, Pete did not chew the shoes.

Pete Moss loved Jane and Doug and they loved him. Repairs on our house were done in a couple of months and we were able to move back home.

A big move

The following year, Bill's company transferred him to Houston. We packed up our home and Pete

Moss, and started a new adventure there. It was challenging, with new jobs, new people, learning a new city, and finding a new church, grocery store, etc.

I got a great job at St. Luke's Hospital as director of heart transplant nursing. We found a rental home in a neighborhood off Dairy Ashford Road and Westheimer Road. For Pete Moss, it was a small fenced-in back yard in the city, which meant no free-roaming the neighborhood. He was so happy when we came home for walks or jogs or just being with him. It did not take Pete long, however, to figure out how to be happy during the day while we were at work. Remember, Pete Moss was a digger!

He dug until he could fit his entire body under the fence! Exploring the neighborhood, he brought home other dog friends. He apparently taught his new friends how to dig and helped them with the task. The posse would travel around the neighborhood during the day.

We did not know what he was doing at first since he was digging out of the side, roaming, returning in the original hole under the fence, and was napping on the back porch when we got home. One day, we arrived home from work to find him sitting on the front step with his friends. After searching, we found the hole.

"Pete, did you dig this hole?" I asked.

His German Shepherd ears slanted backwards, his head slightly turned to the right, pretending he was not there or better yet did not hear a word.

"Pete, did you dig this hole?" I repeated.

Keeping his ears at a slant, he put his head down and laid near the hole, nose covered with dirt.

"Pete, no! You are not supposed to dig holes, OK?" By that time, he was belly-up looking for a rub.

We filled in the hole and with advice from a co-worker we placed cayenne pepper around the filled hole, hoping he would not dig again.

Words from the past rang in my head, "You can't break a digger."

Pete stayed in the yard for a couple of days until he found another area to dig, and he escaped and found his friends. After several of these occasions, most of our back yard was dug up and then filled in.

The far side of our property had a shared fence with the president of the Homeowner's Neighborhood Association, a fact we did not know at the time. This guy had an A+ decorated yard with flower beds filled with bulbs and decorative hardware. His yard could have been on the cover of a garden magazine.

Pete Moss dug on the back-side fence area and escaped into the pristine back yard of the president. Even with that, he was still blocked in and unable to get to the street. I guess that is why he dug another man-sized hole through yet another flower bed! He had finally figured out how to get to his dog friends and be free to roam.

We came home to find Pete Moss on the front porch with lots of dirt on his face and paws. We ran to the back yard to see what he had done. The president's yard was a disaster. Flowers and bulbs were strewn everywhere! Then our doorbell rang. There stood the president of the HNA, and he was livid!

Bill quickly ordered fresh dirt and mulch for the neighbor's yard along with a truckload of apologies. I picked up more cayenne pepper, which washes away with rain, so this was a temporary fix.

Next time, he dug out from the back and ended up in our front yard. This time, however, the neighbor across the street, Alice, called Pete's name when she saw him. She knew our challenges with keeping him in the fenced area. She loved him and he loved her, so when she called him to her yard he went without hesitation. She gave him a fussing and told him to come into her house and stay with her "until your Mommy and Daddy get home." Alice called me at work and reported the catch.

"Don't worry about him, he is watching soap operas with me today," she said.

From that day forward, any time Pete Moss dug out, he went to Alice's house. She would let him in, and they would spend the day together. Pete Moss and Alice were a great combo. I am forever grateful to her.

Recovery companion

Prior to the Houston move, I had a couple of procedures done in Lafayette for infertility. The MD recommended a specialist in Houston to review my case. This resulted in an extensive surgery with five to seven days of recovery in the hospital.

In the hospital, on post-op day two, I was worried about Pete Moss. Bill and Mom were caring for me and Pete Moss was at home not eating much. I asked the surgeon if I could go home earlier than expected so my dog would start eating. Initially, he said no and looked at me like I had two heads, then he smiled and said, "We'll see." It was a rough surgery, but I was walking and eating well. Overall, I was hopeful and ready to go home.

The surgeon later determined I could go home *if* I carefully followed all the mobility, medication, activity and care plans he included in the discharge plan.

"OK, whatever you say, Doc. Just let me go home and see my dog."

When I got home, Pete Moss smelled the bandages and hospital aromas that came with me. He gingerly escorted me from the car to the sofa and lay at my side that day and for weeks to follow. It was as if he knew the discharge plan was to rest. He was also thrilled to be in the air-conditioned house during the summer heat.

While recuperating, I walked slowly and had a pillow over my incisional area. Each day, I increased my walking time and speed. Pete followed me around from room to room, knowing that something was off. He walked with a limp, imitating my movements. Dogs are so precious as they adjust their movements to our rhythms.

As my mobility and stance improved, so did Pete's. I was amazed at how he was so perceptive in my recovery movements. He was one happy dog when I was able to increase walking time and gradually return to running and bike riding. Dogs, I would come to understand, love routine.

* * * * *

Bill's dad, Doug, was diagnosed with cancer at the end of the summer, and subsequently had surgery and radiation therapy. We traveled home each weekend to spend time with Doug and Jane. Bill soon requested a work transfer back to Lafayette to be with his family. Pete Moss wanted to be with everyone as well.

Doug died before we were approved for the transfer. When the approval finally came, we moved home to live with Jane until we could find a home of our own.

We were so sad about Doug's death, yet relieved to be moving home and closer to Jane and our family. While Houston was a good career experience for both of us, we missed our friends and country living. On moving day, we loaded up our baggage and all of Pete's toys. He was sitting up in the back seat of the car with his ears up. I could see him in my rear view as I drove down I-10 east bound. Pete was more excited than anyone to be in the car and off to another adventurous place.

After a few months in Lafayette, we bought a

half-built abandoned home in Milton, a suburb of Lafayette. It was in the country with three acres of land and not many houses around. It was much like the place we had prior to the Houston move. It had space for us, and Pete Moss could roam the fields again.

He was still a puppy in so many ways, sometimes barking at the full moon all night and sleeping all day. He hid from thunder and made his way into any air-conditioned space he could. Sometimes he got into trouble by snooping around in places he should not. He was bitten by a snake once, but after being treated for the swelling he did well.

He found his way to a nearby farm that had fighting roosters. These are well-fed, trained animals that are worth quite a lot of money if they should win a fight. I am not a fan of this fighting, nor did I know much about it. I had no idea someone down the road owned one of these fighting roosters until Pete Moss came home bleeding from gun shots of rock salt pellets. We were told who shot him and that Pete Moss had probably gotten too close to the rooster cages.

Our poor pet was bleeding and filled with pellet holes, so it was back to the vet. Pete Moss survived, never ventured back to that farm, and we fenced in the yard.

Fence or not, somehow dogs find a way to get into mischief. After all, what could be more fun than finding a pack of dog friends to travel with or just running around the property?

* * * * *

One Christmas holiday I ordered some terrific, packaged muffins for gifts. I was making baskets of goodies and ordered a case of various flavors. Each of the 12 packs had four muffins. My favorite flavors were sourdough and cheddar cheese, but I also ordered blueberry and oatmeal muffins.

Arriving home from work, I discovered the box on the front porch. It was open, not chewed or torn, and had 11 packs of muffins instead of the 12 I had ordered. The missing pack was cheddar cheese. Since there were no teeth marks or tearing on the box, I figured someone down the road may have been hungry, so I let go of tracking down a muffin thief.

"Did you see anyone come today and take the muffins?" I asked Pete.

He turned his head sideways as if to say, "What did you say?"

I let it go.

Two months after Christmas, Bill and I dug a hole for a new Japanese Magnolia tree in the back yard. The base was large, and, digging two feet down, Bill's shovel hit something. It was a full four-pack of cheddar cheese muffins in the original bag, uneaten. We both smiled but were amazed that Pete Moss had opened our Christmas box, taken a four-pack of muffins and buried it this deep without us knowing.

We looked at Pete Moss, sunning in the back yard with us.

"Pete, did you bury these muffins?"

His head shifted inquisitively, and his ears were parallel to the ground. He rolled over for a belly rub.

A found mate

One Sunday in October of 1991, Bill and I were watching football when Pete began barking as if to call us to the door. I went outside and Pete just stared at me, turning his head to the right as if to say, "Look over there, I found a friend!" There, in the Liriope bed, lay a sweet puppy, scared, shaking and adorable. Pete's little friend had obviously not been cared for as he showed signs of severe neglect and abuse. He was quite dirty and skinny with his bones visible. He blinked his eyes as though I was going to yell or chase him away. I gradually approached him, and he sunk further into the Liriope bed. As I reached over to pet him, he immediately ran off to sit in another flower bed!

I opened the door to the house and yelled.

"Bill, there's a puppy out here. He looks scared. Come see."

Bill looked at him fondly and said, "Hey, puppy, you are precious. It's going to be OK." And then he turned to me.

"If we can't find the owner and you feed him or her, you know we will have another dog," Bill said.

We initially named him orphan Annie, but found out later that Annie was really a male puppy, so we changed the name to Andy. He was a beautiful light-colored Golden Retriever who seemed to be about six months old. He was so sweet and grateful to be at our home. It was obvious that he had not been cared for, so we took him to the vet for a checkup.

We discovered that he had ringworms and heartworms, a BB stuck in his nose, and probably had been beaten as a puppy. A heartbreaking story for this young dog looking for love and a home. Pete knew it, and he loved Andy from the start.

After feeding him, bathing him, taking him to the vet, and searching for his owner with "Lost Dog" signs for a few weeks, we received no calls. So we decided he was ours.

After he found Andy, Pete relaxed more and let Andy do most of the barking and watching. They were a great team, and I had many thoughts that two dogs were easier than one because they were always playing with each other or sleeping together. Of course, they were also double the trouble at times.

Lost Pete

Family and friends would help us with the dogs when we had to leave town or were busy at work. One time when Pete Moss was at Jane's house, he caught sight of a runner and ran with him as he did with Bill and me. He got lost, however, and was unable to find his way home.

Jane felt awful. We had been out of town, and when we returned we moved into high gear to find him. It was a rough 10 days. We put up signs, sent emails and made phone calls. We got word of sightings on both sides of town, so we recruited many people to search the streets for Pete.

A guy named André had seen one of the signs with Pete's picture at our mutual friends' house. A few days later André was driving through town when he saw a German Shepherd wandering the street. Slowing down, he realized this dog looked just like the dog in the sign he saw, so he opened the car door. The wandering dog, looking tired and hungry, stopped to look in the car. André called out, "Pete?" and the dog turned his head in response.

André had pizza in the car, lured him in with a piece, and drove over to our friends' who then called us. You can only imagine how excited we were! We made a mad dash to pick up our sweet pet, Pete Moss. He was tired and hungry and stunk. We could not believe we found him. The lesson learned: Do not give up when they are lost!

Pete Moss was getting up in years, and being lost probably stressed and aged him a bit. He was slowing down. Andy kept an eye on him as running and chasing became challenging for Pete.

Later that year, we took him for his annual checkup and routine exam. Pete was 15 years old and had begun to eat less, had developed cataracts, and was having trouble walking. The vet confirmed that Pete was getting close to the end of a well-lived life. We could care for him as long as he had the quality of being himself. When he began to have bowel and bladder problems, the vet encouraged us to consider calling him when we thought it was time.

We really did not want to put him to sleep, though we did not want him to suffer, so we decided that around Easter we would have the vet put him to rest. We did not commit to a day.

A few weeks later, one early morning Andy was barking incessantly outside. Pete Moss had fallen into the pool. I jumped in fully clothed to get him but it was too late.

Wrapping him in a blanket, we buried him. The guilt I felt from his death weighed heavily on me for years. I wondered when we should have taken him to the vet so he could have had a more peaceful death.

Bill knew exactly how to bury a dog. I called work to take off for a few hours, and it was an incredibly sad day. We made a cross for his grave from pecan tree branches.

My sweet dog, Pete. I have dreamt about him many times over the years. I look at his pictures and smile. Having a dog like Pete for 15 years was amazing and burying him was difficult. I learned about a dog's love and never imagined the grief associated with losing a pet.

Through the next year, Andy was our comfort. While Andy grieved some, he moved into first place. First place meant Andy became an inside dog with air conditioning and got 100 percent of the attention.

Following Pete Moss's death, I attended a conference and there was a class developed by graduate students in psychology. The title was something related to pet loss and human relationships with their animals. The title piqued my curiosity, since I was still grieving for Pete, so I signed up.

The class was full, with more than 20 students. We introduced ourselves and our pets. The class had one focus, and that was to talk a bit about what our pets meant to us. I will never forget that experience, especially the unmistakable empathy among all in attendence.

Chapter 3

Andy

80 pounds of sweetness
(October 1991 – April 2006)

Andy was one of Pete Moss's finds after one of his morning doggy-rounds in the neighborhood. He was a golden brown, matted, stinky and muddy dog who looked like he had never had a bath. His coloring was golden blond with white highlights around his eyes and face. He shivered and squinted his eyes in fear. He probably thought that we would chase him away, but from that day on, we loved him.

He was an extremely sick and underweight little puppy with parasites. It was obvious that he had been shot and was left with one partially blind eye and a permanent BB stuck in his nose. The vet said that he was a lucky little dog to find us, but we felt we were the lucky ones. He bounced back from all of the treatments, got healthy, and quickly joined in the family routine for daily runs. Andy and Pete Moss loved the adventurous new smells or sights for the day. Andy was all about living in the moment.

He was our first Golden Retriever. A permanent happy face, he was always smiling and wagging his tail – even in his sleep. If someone was not a dog lover, he was not pushy. He sat by their feet until they came around and gave him a pet.

One Saturday afternoon, we invited friends and family over for a barbeque and swimming. We took lots of family photos in various poses around the yard for keepsakes. When we got the pictures developed and looked through the pack, Andy was in every photo! He had the same pose, same smile, same quiet and gentle presence. We later named the day "An Afternoon with Andy."

While sweet and kind, he also had a mischievous side, but somehow his contrite happy eyebrows and smile often got him a "get out of jail free" card. We believe that every dog needs some training and discipline, so when he chewed on furniture or dug a hole, we called him out on it. His nickname, when he was in trouble, was "Randy."

* * * * *

Andy had a fun life with his older brother Pete Moss as they roamed the neighborhood each morning and afternoon. They loved to chase rabbits, run squirrels up a tree, or sniff out possums, raccoons or other country animals. They barked at the moon, and when it was full, they barked all night. They stayed cool in the hot summer months by seeking shade under a tree to nap. Andy really liked digging holes so that he was sitting in cool dirt or mud. He also liked to move mulch out of the way to dig a crisp hole!

When Andy was the proper age, we had him neutered. We talked to the vet about the surgery and

Andy

Once when I had packed for a business trip and was about to take off, Andy jumped into the trunk of my car next to my luggage. It was almost as if he was saying, "Mom, I want to go, too!" (What dog doesn't want to go for a ride at every opportunity?)

planned to have Andy stay overnight with the vet since he was under so many treatments to get healthy. The surgery went well, but was more extensive than usual. An exploratory surgery was needed to find the hidden testicle in his abdominal area.

Within the first post-op day at home, Andy chewed through the plastic Elizabethan collar. After buying a new one and getting him set, he got that one stuck to the base of a tree within minutes, so we had to purchase a third collar!

Dog tails

Andy, like Pete, loved to find a dog in need and bring it home. One evening, we heard what sounded like someone dragging chains followed by a bark. We went out to the driveway only to find Andy with a new friend, a beautiful black lab who had escaped his home and had come to visit us. We found out that his name was Lucky and brought him back to his proper owner. It was the beginning of a new friendship for the dogs.

When not running around with Pete Moss or Lucky, or on a jog with us, Andy enjoyed naps with a fan on his face and sleeping next to his best friends. He would sleep anywhere! Sometimes, he would get locked in the garage without us knowing, as he did not wake up to the sound of the door. He may have also had a hearing problem!

In addition to digging holes, Andy was quite competent at burying bones. One afternoon, he quietly went to the back yard with one of his chew bones and buried it, unaware that we were watching him. After the proper bone burial, his paws crafted an incredible dirt cover and pushed leaves over it for extra coverage.

He walked back to the porch never realizing that we were watching him. It must be tiring work to dig and hide bones as it seemed to bring on nap time. We often wondered how many bones were buried in our yard.

A thorny obstacle

Andy had an extra special love for sticks. He "shopped" for good sticks in the back yard, bringing them to us like gifts. We called it "stick shopping." He also obviously liked to eat sticks, which we did not know about until one scary day.

He was at our back doorstep not barking, not moving his head and sitting with a quiet gentle stare straight ahead. He would not wag his tail or move his head to our voice. He would not eat a treat or drink water and we knew he loved both. We thought that maybe he was bitten by a snake, though we saw no wounds on his body. Then the nurse in me thought that he might have a brain tumor. We could not get him to do anything.

We called the vet and loaded him up for the stressful ride, not knowing if our dog was dying. Richard, our veterinarian, checked him and could not get a wag, head movement or bark. He checked

Andy's body, ears and eyes. When he opened Andy's mouth, he said, "Wait a minute, I'll be right back." He came back with long forceps, and with Andy's mouth propped open and head held by the tech, he gently pulled out a 7-inch rose bush branch, with thorns. At that moment, Andy started looking around, barking for a treat and wagging his tail. Lucky us and lucky dog.

A new adventure

Andy had been lonely since Pete Moss died, and then Lucky moved away. Even though we were still grieving a bit for Pete, we decided to get another dog. At the time, we were both working full-time, and I was also in graduate school. The thought of training another puppy was not at the top of my list.

Once we made the decision to get a second dog, we knew that we wanted a German Shepherd or a pound puppy that might be part German Shepherd. We loved the combination of having a German Shepherd and Golden Retriever since Pete Moss and Andy were such a great team. We spread the word that we were looking, and one of the pharmacists where I worked shared the news that her German Shepherd had eight puppies that we could look at in a few weeks.

When I told Bill, he said, "Great. But you know we don't 'just visit' puppies and leave. One of them is going to look at us in just the right way, as if choosing us, and we will bring him or her home."

In October of 2000, we drove out to the country to look at the puppies – with a towel, a toy, and a clean kennel, just in case. One of the puppies "chose us" and we named him Buddy that afternoon. He was an adorable, purebred German Shepherd with mostly black with gold markings. As a 6- to 8-week-old puppy, Buddy was mostly fur and ran like a little black bear. Big paws, big ears and a big chewer.

The first night we brought him home, we played with him and fed him, trying to wear him out so he would sleep quietly in his cage. Buddy did not sleep the first, second, or third night. He yapped and cried. Those first few nights without his mom or pack were tough for the little guy, not to mention what the new puppy sounds did to Andy.

Andy moved out to the front yard, under the large red oak tree, to get away from the noise. We could not get Andy to come near the house for a few days. He slowly came to the front porch and gradually to the back porch. We brought his food to him until he could adjust to Buddy.

Andy worked his way back into the house and lay close to the puppy kennel, but when Buddy yapped, he walked away. After about 10 days, they were in the same room. Buddy wanted to jump all over Andy all the time, biting or sucking on his ears, waking him up from naps and barking at him. Over time, Andy realized that Buddy needed love. As he grew, Andy accepted the new world order. They played and slept next to each other, shared or stole each other's toys and became best friends.

Buddy was quite keen about being protective of us and watching for anyone that came near our property. His sense of smell was incredible. He was always sniffing and checking both Andy and us. I guess he wanted to make sure we were OK.

Two smart dogs in the house were comforting and fun to watch. Once Buddy surpassed Andy in weight and height, he took over the house. Andy did not seem to mind. He did whatever Buddy wanted to do. They would take each other's toys and run around the yard for hours.

Andy's sense of presence and need to comfort family was his special gift, while Buddy protected the world.

Constant companion

Andy did not like to see a suitcase come out of the attic. One month, I had a couple of work trips. For the first one, I laid my open suitcase on the floor while gathering my clothes and toiletries to pack. Andy crawled into my suitcase to take a nap! Maybe he wanted to come.

Within a few days of returning from that trip, I had another meeting in New Orleans. This time, Andy skipped the nap and jumped into the open car trunk and sat next to the suitcase!

* * * * *

Andy loved Jane, my mother-in-law, and would warm her feet by sitting on her shoes when she visited. When Jane was diagnosed with pancreatic cancer, Andy paid extra attention to her. He could sense that something was wrong, stayed with her whenever he could and was with her when she died. He loved her and she loved him.

About seven months after Jane died, Buddy began to smell Andy's belly. Gently approaching Andy, he would smell the left side of Andy's belly, give him a lick and look at us. Buddy seemed to hover over Andy several days in a row. It was time for Andy's vet checkup, and we shared the story about Buddy going to the same location on Andy's belly to smell.

The vet told us that many dogs sense when something is off and did in fact find a cancerous tumor in Andy's belly. It was spreading to his other organs and became inoperable. Andy was 15 years old. This was a tough one for us as Bill's dad and mom had both died from cancer.

While there were no surgical treatments, there were medications for inflammation and pain that worked well for Andy, and, of course, canned food, chicken bites and more. Andy did not seem to be bothered by the tumor. He slept a little more, but continued to eat, play and act normally for a few months.

One day, however, after a little outside romp, he walked into the dining room and would not eat or drink. Andy was ready to die. After talking with the vet, he offered to put Andy to sleep at the office or come to our home. We told him that we would care for him at home and call him when it was time.

We, the family, cared for him around the clock for the next 48 hours. He was watched and loved on by everyone. Not eating or drinking, he slept and let us pet him. We talked to him and played his favorite music. Once he lost his ability to stand and go pee, we called the vet. Andy was tired and barely opened his eyes. The vet came to our home and gently put him to sleep.

It was a terribly sad day, and I still cry when I think about it.

Bill and our neighbor, Jerry, wrapped Andy in his favorite yellow blanket and gave him the proper burial at Paw Hill, the same area on our property where we buried Pete Moss. They dug a large, deep hole and gently placed our sweet furbaby Andy there. We placed lime all around the hole.

We let Buddy come out on the property during the burial to see the process. We thought that maybe this would help him understand. Buddy tried to get in the hole with Andy – which made our crying worse. We knew that Buddy would be lost without him.

A great dog who lived an incredible 15 years, Andy died one year and one day after Jane, his beloved friend and "grandmother."

To say goodbye to Andy, our first Golden Retriever, was like losing the physical presence of love. It was difficult to grieve a second dog that lived to be 15.

We were sad and so was Buddy.

Chapter 4

Buddy

Dog-Wonder
(October 2000 – July 2012)

Buddy was a beautiful puppy with nearly 80 percent black fur and gold accents on his eyebrows, paws and belly. He kept most of his black coat as he aged, though he began graying later in life. He was born with huge paws and ears, eventually growing into them.

Buddy, as a puppy, wanted to lie on Andy all the time. He insisted on sleeping with Andy and chewing on his ears. Once sweet old Andy accepted Buddy, he was Buddy's pillow for life.

Buddy was a crazy and noisy puppy for a few months. He was a chewer who left permanent marks in chairs, table legs and other pieces of furniture.

Besides that, Buddy chewed, played or slept with a ball for the whole time we had him. His nickname was "Ball Dog." He practiced rolling a ball with his paw with enough power to pop it into the air and catch it in his mouth. He practiced all day long. If he popped it in the pool, he would not fetch it because he did not like to swim. Instead, he would stare at it, then at us, bark, and finally wait for us to get the ball.

When he was not flipping it in the air with his

"power paw," he brought the ball to anyone available to play fetch with him. He particularly liked us to throw the ball on the roof. He would watch it bounce when it rolled down, then jump to catch it in midair. He was addicted to balls.

He would smell and examine everyone who came to our yard or the neighbor's property. He was extremely smart and always knew where his balls were, so he could prevent another dog from retrieving them.

Living up to his name

Buddy became good friends with our neighbors and felt so comfortable with them that he took their possessions — soccer balls, basketballs, shoes, outdoor candles, clothing and more. He would bring the "borrowed" goods to our side yard, where he would sit and enjoy all of his treasures. When we returned the items, we often had to purchase replacements for what he had chewed up. The neighbors were more than kind to this wildly curious dog.

One sunny afternoon, I was walking him in the neighborhood and two boys, whom I did not know, were playing basketball in their front yard. Buddy saw them bouncing the ball and immediately wanted to join. As he ran toward them, they dropped the ball and ran away. Buddy grabbed the ball and ran home. He had punctured it, so we immediately bought a new basketball for the boys.

Buddy became friends with my work colleagues,

Buddy

attending the annual heart run and other events at the hospital where I worked. He was not a magnet for the soft at heart as he tended to bark at anyone who might possess the "I am scared of German Shepherds" scent.

* * * * *

Buddy was a large built German Shepherd. His size alone commanded respect. One friend called him "large and in charge." Because of his size, we took him to training classes. For nearly six months we worked with the trainer to teach him the required tasks and commands. The trainer was world-renowned for training police dogs. He gave us exercises to practice, which we did, but all Buddy wanted to do was play ball. The training partially worked, but head strong Buddy, and his owners, did not always follow through with the training. He did learn to sit on command, but *not* to stay.

If I threw Buddy a ball, he retrieved it, played with it a bit and then returned it at my feet to repeat the process. If a friend or family member visited, he followed the same process to recruit more arms to throw. He did this for hours!

We also bought a machine that would automatically pitch balls at a certain frequency. As they shot out of the machine Buddy loved retrieving them and returning them to us. He would lay the ball down, back up, sit and stare until we put the ball back into the machine to keep the game going. Once he figured out this ball-throwing machine, he thought he would be smart and get the ball right out of the shoot, which he soon learned was not a wise thing to do! We did not replace the automatic pitching machine when it broke.

* * * * *

After Andy died, Buddy hung out with the neighbors' dogs — Big Shot, Ben and Chessie. His favorite friend was Chessie, a smaller dog that was quick and could run fast. Buddy and Chessie would sit together in the yard on the corner or sit in their respective yards watching the cars go by. Some cars and trucks warranted a full-on chase with barking by both.

In the mornings, these neighborhood dogs would roam around, checking out various rabbit holes or possum scents in the acreage around our homes. Many of these animals did not survive the dog posse.

Buddy in charge

We lived on a gravel road, so it was easy to hear car tires, and the dogs never missed an opportunity to bark or chase. Bicycles were an extra challenge, and apologies go to anyone who was chased by Buddy and his boys.

One summer, our gravel road was transformed into a paved road. The construction crew was on site for a few months, surveying, setting up, paving, creating ditches and more. Buddy was the "foreman" of this project. He would leave after breakfast and stay with the crew until we returned from work.

Andy was not enamored with the job site, so he often watched, or pretended to, or napped.

When Andy died, Buddy was six years old and missed him. Even though Buddy had neighborhood friends, it was not long before we decided to get another Golden Retriever. We searched kennels and asked around for anyone who may have a Golden Retriever or mixed breed. AJ joined the family later, in 2007.

Buddy easily accepted AJ, and he let him know who was in charge! If the new pup tried to get one of his toys, Buddy would gently put his large mouth around AJ's entire head. AJ loved this game. He thought Buddy was his mom.

AJ quickly liked the ball game and began to take Buddy's balls when he was down for a nap. Once Buddy woke up, the chase was on to get his balls back. This went on for years. AJ was a great swimmer, so if Buddy popped his ball in the pool, AJ swam with the ball in his mouth until Buddy barked at him.

When we threw the ball to Buddy, AJ would take off to get it before him. They wrestled and whoever got the ball was chased by the other. Round and round bushes, through the trees, and into mud and water, they chased each other until they got tired.

Medical emergency

In the summer of 2010, we had what seemed like a normal Saturday afternoon working in the yard and playing ball with Buddy. After supper, he was restless and seemed to want to throw up but could not. We ended up bringing him to the vet, who quickly examined and X-rayed Buddy. "Stomach flip" was the diagnosis, which is most often fatal and more common for large-breed animals. The official term is bloat or stomach torsion. We had never had a dog with bloat.

In the ER, the vet explained the percentage of dogs that do not survive unless diagnosed early. She was preparing us for the worst while explaining the surgery and giving us information. We signed the papers for surgery and prayed for the best. Some hours later, around 2:00 a.m., Buddy not only survived the surgery, but he immediately stood up in the small cage and started barking. He began to pull out his IV and so he had to be collared. Within a few hours, he was eating canned dog food and man-made meatballs and barking at the vet techs again. We were elated. We were so grateful to our vets for a quick diagnosis and successful surgery.

We took him home on a collar with instructions for limited activity and food restrictions. Buddy, like all of our dogs, tried everything to get that collar off of his neck. Having a large dog recover after an abdominal surgery is a challenge.

Keeping him down and quiet for six weeks was not easy. He recovered well and returned to his exercise, ball-playing and hanging out with AJ. We got him a small blow-up kid's pool to lay in and cool off. We also curtailed ball-playing and running for an hour before and after meals. We paid attention to the heat and let Buddy stay in the air-conditioned house on hot summer days.

* * * * *

Two years later, on May 1, 2012, Buddy, who was 11 years and 9 months old, was not acting right. He was tired and would not eat or drink anything. His eyes were saying he felt bad and wanted to be left alone. He tried to walk to his water bowl and could not, choosing instead to lie down by the oven, which was not a corner that he normally frequented. His big brown eyes were sad and his beautiful shepherd ears were at half-mast. This behavior made us wonder if this might be his last day. His little brother, AJ, tried to comfort him.

Off to the vet's office we went. His gums were pale, which, with no external signs of bleeding, meant he was bleeding internally. After X-rays he was diagnosed with Hemangiosarcoma with a bleeding tumor on his spleen. We thought that he was going to die immediately, and it was scary. I cried and tried to keep quiet so Buddy would not be any sadder. The lab work revealed a blood count of 50 percent of what it should be. If he were not operated on that day, he would die, and chances were high that he may die in surgery.

Our vet recommended immediate transport to LSU Veterinary Animal Hospital in Baton Rouge to have him evaluated for surgery. Off we went, placing

Buddy on our favorite Budweiser blanket on the back seat. He covered his face with his paws and slept lifelessly the entire one-hour drive. I sang to him to soothe him. Barely able to walk into the building, he collapsed once inside and was immediately evaluated by the oncology team with more X-rays for other tumors or problems. The surgical team evaluated all tests to determine the next steps and prepared him and us for surgery.

It was determined that he had no other tumors; however, they explained that the tumor may be malignant. He was dehydrated, but a good candidate for surgery. We kissed and hugged him and told him that we loved him and off he went to surgery. They planned to keep him for a few days, so once the plan was in place and Buddy was in their hands, they suggested we go home until they called us. The drive home was quiet and tearful.

He not only survived the surgery but began to show his personality by standing up in his cage and trying to remove his collar and the IV in his leg. His bark had returned. The LSU vet hospital staff called our home with updates at least three times a day, sometimes more often when we requested. The technicians told us they would go to his cage and give him some "sugar" so he would not be lonely.

Buddy spent two days at the animal hospital. He was not eating or drinking much. The staff believed Buddy would not eat since he was away from his family, so they cleared him for discharge. It was a happy day.

Once Buddy saw us, he wagged his tail, picked up his head and began drinking and eating – in that order. At home, he still tried to remove his collar, which we expected from him. He never liked collars. I am sure he joins the ranks of many dogs who figured out how to chew, remove or destroy the E-Collar.

* * * * *

The week after surgery, we got the biopsy results from the removed tumor and found out that it was cancer. Survival for this type of cancer is two to four months or four to six months with treatment of either IV chemotherapy or the chemo pill. Intravenous chemotherapy, Plan A, involves high risks including possible death as a complication, possible overnight stays at the animal hospital and x-rays. Chemotherapy by mouth, Plan B, is lower risk, no overnight stays, blood work once a month and is the least expensive route. We chose Plan B so Buddy could enjoy his time at home in his own back yard with us and AJ.

When he got home, he was weak and in need of strengthening. He slept with the ball next to him, licking it and probably dreaming of his ball-playing days. He also enjoyed the new canned food options. Before surgery, canned dog food was saved for Christmas, special occasions and birthdays. He was treated gently by his brother AJ, and once mobile they returned to their old hi-jinks, chasing each other and running after cats and squirrels in the back yard.

He was one lucky dog, and we were so blessed and grateful for the vet care in Lafayette and Baton Rouge. Buddy was back, albeit not forever. We were particularly grateful to Cole Sandow, a vet student at LSU, who taught us how important it was to "sugar up" the dogs that are ill and suffering.

While the prognosis was not as long as we had hoped, every moment with Buddy was special. He was himself, large and in charge! AJ stayed with Buddy, letting him lead as long as he lived. If Buddy were to sit and rest, AJ did the same or stayed nearby.

* * * * *

In late July, Buddy began showing the late stages of his life. He was tired and moving slowly. There was nothing else we could do for him but love him, and that we did. He was treated with anti-inflammatory and pain medications which helped him. When he got to the point of not being able to walk, the vet came to our home to put him to sleep.

Buddy was so tired and in no pain but did get a last look into our eyes for what felt like a peaceful goodbye.

As with the other dogs, Bill and our neighbor, Jerry, dug the hole at Paw Hill. We had named this section of land "Paw Hill" because it was the location where Pete Moss and Andy had been buried.

Four days after his death, I journaled profound feelings of sadness and heartfelt gratitude. The vacillation of love and pain. If you love, really love, there will be suffering and sadness when death occurs.

The house was quiet. Every room had a reminder of Buddy. I missed him staring at me while I was on the phone or barking like a crazy dog when the doorbell rang or when a delivery truck arrived.

Love and Life. Death and Dying. Joy and Pain. Grief and Memories. We cannot avoid it.

All would be well. Thank you, Lord, for sending me Buddy to teach me so much about love and loss.

Chapter 5

Chief of Hospitality
(December 2006 – August 2017)

In 2006, someone referred me to a Golden Retriever breeder. I gave him a call and learned that his puppies were going to be born in October. So, when the mom delivered 12 healthy little bundles of fur, I *had* to see them. Oh, my goodness, I had never seen 12 puppies in a large bucket, all trying to get out as they stepped on each other.

I wanted all of them! They were so cute making those puppy sounds, eyes barely open and ready to test their little teeth on my finger. Making the selection was easy. The one with a little white spot on his neck, surrounded by beautiful golden fur was irresistible. The breeder said that the puppies would be weaned from their mom and ready for pick up in early December.

I have to say, it was fun to prepare the house for the little wiggle worm. I was in the process of leaving my 16-year full-time job as a hospital nurse executive to work part-time and help my parents in their aging. I also was excited about having time to help our new puppy and Buddy acclimate and transition back to having two dogs in the house.

On a cool December evening, I drove to meet the breeder to pick up AJ, Andy Junior, named after our first Golden Retriever. He had a red ribbon around his neck and looked like a little Christmas present. He had big soft paws, soft ears and a full little belly from his recent feeding. He was full of energy and crawling out of the bucket to be held.

After hugging and playing with him, it was time to head home. I had a nice-sized box with a towel in my car, and carefully placed him in the box on the back seat. I was a half-mile down the road when AJ started yapping and climbing out of the box. He crawled over everything to get to me, where he sat and chewed on my elbow.

Why didn't I get a dog carrier? What was I thinking?

I pulled over into a parking lot to avoid getting into a wreck. He was trying to get in my lap or on the floorboard by my feet and kept moving like a noodle. I forgot what puppyhood was like. I should have remembered this from our last puppy!

I moved the box to the front passenger side, belted it in, and put my right hand in the box to hold him down. It was a rough ride home, focusing on driving and listening to him cry. I told myself to just drive slowly and get home safely.

Once we arrived home, AJ made himself right at home. Buddy welcomed him, even though he had to push his big German Shepherd "in charge" weight

AJ

The boy liked to play...and fetch.

around to get that puppy into shape.

* * * * *

My daily routine includes morning prayers and journaling. AJ enjoyed joining me by chewing on my journal each morning, leaving a nice set of teeth marks in the cover.

For the first few weeks I carried him around like luggage. When AJ got too wiggly or began moving where he was not supposed to, Buddy would either put his paw out to stop him or place the puppy's head in his mouth to quiet him. AJ just loved anything that Buddy did.

AJ slept in his cage at first, but after a few months he outgrew it. We got another cage, which he also outgrew, but the bigger problem was that he wanted to live in the house with Buddy. He would wake us up each night by crying or barking until Buddy, Bill, or I went out to the cage to acknowledge him. Once the kennel door was open, he bolted out and either ran to his food bowl or jumped on top of Buddy.

Adapting to country life

Living in the country is a perfect setting for big dogs. There are bugs, lizards, squirrels, and birds in the trees to watch, along with many home projects in which for AJ to get involved.

I had just gotten a used pottery wheel to start making pottery at home. We opened up some space in the garage, and I began teaching myself wheel-throwing techniques. AJ loved to watch the mud/ clay go around the wheel and thought it was a game. He would try to – and sometimes did – bite the clay while it was spinning. I am not the best potter in the world, but having a dog contribute to my projects was not helpful. He eventually got tired watching the wheel and hearing me say, "No, AJ."

Unlike the German Shepherds we owned that never liked to swim, I should have prepared myself for AJ, also known as "Water Dog." In early February, when he was four months old, he jumped right into the ice-cold pool. I was scared that he would drown and as I ran to grab him, he came up for air swimming in rhythm, smiling and looking for us. We got him out and toweled him dry. He instantly took the towel into the yard to rip it up, overjoyed at his new experience.

AJ and Buddy were intrigued with anything moving and looked to each other to find something to do. AJ poked around for anything to catch, from mosquitos in the air to possums under the deck. Squirrels and racoons, he found, were not a good idea to chase in the yard, though he had a grand time going after rabbits. Buddy would scan and smell the fence line each morning and evening.

AJ loved Buddy's toys. He would take Buddy's ball and then the chase was on. They chased each other around the yard for hours – hiding in a bush, coming out, resting, then starting all over again.

We taught AJ the basic commands such as "sit,"

"lay" and "shake hands," but he never mastered "stay." AJ thought the better game was to run and get chased, so he made every little game a chase. It was his sport for life.

* * * * *

While it is quiet in the country, the road in front of our house, once paved, had cars driving relatively fast. AJ always wanted to go across the street, but we never wanted to chance a car hitting him. Most of his life he was behind the backyard fence. If we dared to open the fence, he was off and running, making it a challenge to corral him. We had good neighbors, however, who were always ready to help us get him home.

Once fully grown, AJ was a solid 80-pound dog with beautiful and fluffy reddish-blond fur. Not a lap dog by size, he believed he should be one. His large paws were soft with fur sticking up between his toes and he walked quietly. His ears were as soft as velvet and his big brown eyes would make people melt – probably because of his expressive eyebrows.

He loved to come quietly around the corner, pop his neck and ears up, cock his head, and bark for food. Once I made eye contact or a move toward him, he would run to his bowl or begin a game of chase.

When outside he would run needlessly around and around the fenced acreage. It did not matter if he was being chased. The wind in his face, sometimes eyes closed, he ran and ran and ran.

Head strong, body strong and heart strong

AJ was so kind. When I took him to the nursing home to visit my parents and the other residents, he would place his head on their leg or lap and raise his eyes so they could pet him.

When he saw a little child or baby, his endearing qualities came through. Initially, he would get his big head close to the car seat or baby carrier. Once he saw that it was a baby, he would smell it, and then look back at us as if to say, "Do you see this?" We would respond, "It's OK, AJ, but don't lick." He would then lie down near the baby with his tail moving at top speed, and just watch. If the baby did not cry or scream, he would begin the toy exchange. AJ would smell the baby again, give the baby one of his toys, and then try to take one of the baby's toys. He would scrunch his little nose for the baby and, if possible, get awfully close so the baby could touch his nose. When the parent let AJ stay close, he would sit quietly or sleep next to the baby.

* * * * *

We bought him many toys so that he always had something to chew. He usually "de-stuffed" a soft toy and maybe decapitated it or removed a limb or two. The dog toy box in the closet was filled with mangled toys. AJ would go into the closet, dig around, and return with one of the chewed-up toys hanging out of his mouth.

AJ was a ball of energy and it was usually evening before he finally wore himself out for a nap. Quietly walking around, he would check to see if any part of the sofa was vacant. If someone was on the sofa, he placed his head or feet on whomever was there. AJ was a true lurker. He loved to be near anyone. I could lay on him and he would not move. His nickname became "pillow with a heartbeat."

* * * * *

Praying before meals is our family tradition and we taught our dogs to bow their head while we pray. As soon as we said "Amen," AJ would bark for food.

AJ's friends included Emmie, Lizzy, Lexie and Abby. Abby looked like his twin, and when they rolled in the dirt I could barely tell them apart. I could tell that AJ needed a full-time companion again after Buddy's death.

A new addition

We looked around for a rescue or homeless German Shepherd and eventually found Heidi. She was the perfect new friend for AJ. Heidi was bashful and fearful, having been sheltered and rescued. AJ was full of fun and tried everything to get Heidi to play with him. If she would not play, he would push toys at her nose to get her up and chasing him, albeit short distances.

One hot afternoon in July of 2017, the dogs were inside most of the day for obvious reasons. AJ saw a squirrel and we let him out. He chased it up the tree and returned for air conditioning; however, he seemed to be hobbling back and maybe hurting or limping. He came in the house slowly and stopped without wagging his tail. He laid down with his ears flat like he was hurting.

With our history of Buddy's stomach flip some years prior, we initially called the vet when we could not get AJ to drink water or move. We took him in immediately. X-rays were done and we felt certain we were going to hear the term "stomach flip" again. It was just as bad. AJ had a tumor encompassing his entire abdomen and intestines. The tumor was wrapped around most of the organs. The ER vet petted AJ and consoled us. The best plan was to do an ultrasound and additional tests to determine if the tumor was operable. We took our sweet dog home with inflammation and pain meds and a truck full of love.

He bounced back on steroids and was a real trooper for the next week of ultrasounds and vet visits. After a full week of testing, the tumor was deemed inoperable. Our sweet AJ was facing his final year of life.

Over the next six weeks, the pain medications and steroids helped him to stay active, loving and funny. We focused our time on loving him and enjoying every moment. When he could no longer be himself, we would call the vet to help us say goodbye.

His tumor grew and his belly was swollen, yet he

still loved being around us. In the final days, he cried a bit in his sleep, and his mobility was shrinking. We knew the time was near.

The day finally came on August 16, 2017. Ironically, it was the feast day of St. Roch, a patron saint for dogs. It is said that he contracted a disease and a dog brought him bread and licked his wounds.

AJ, at 10 years and 10 months old, was put to sleep at our home by his vet, Richard.

The decision to call the vet was delayed by us so many times. We did not want him to suffer, yet did not want him to die. AJ was so strong. Despite carrying his large belly, I think he just wanted to please us. It was a terribly hard decision. AJ was even happy to see the vet and vet tech when they arrived on that final day.

Grace and Grief.

I miss my sweet AJ. He was fun, curious, playful, never met a stranger, loved to eat, and was always adventurous.

When he died, part of my life became dull. Having AJ as a pet was a terrific experience. Losing him was just the opposite: extraordinarily sad, difficult and depressing.

AJ was buried, again by Bill and Jerry, in the back part of our property, in Paw Hill. We all cried.

The month that AJ died, I was helping with a grief workshop and caring for my dad, who was dying from Alzheimer's. Life was sad enough. Pet loss came up in discussion as one of the participants wanted to talk about her pet dying. Pet loss was not part of our planning. I needed the therapy also, so I promised myself that when the time came I would try to bring pet grief more to the forefront of healing.

Chapter 6

Heidi
'Enigma Lou'
(January 8, 2014 – present)

In January of 2014, still grieving over Buddy, we decided to get another German Shepherd. Loving the German Shepherd and Golden Retriever combination, we began the search. Their personalities complement ours and each other's. One dog, large and in charge, one dog, large and happy no matter what, and two owners who let them rule the house.

For four months we searched newspapers and animal shelter websites and made inquiries hoping to find a puppy.

One cold morning in January, we drove to a home where two former police force German Shepherds were bred with a resulting litter of 10 puppies. All were gone except for one. The breeder walked us to the puppy area. The puppy, soon to be named Heidi, was unkempt and living in a small cage with a damp muddy floor. Her little space was fenced off from her mother and father, who both barked and growled at us.

The puppy was trying to hide herself in her tiny space with her ears pinned back. She looked so scared and her eyes told us so.

She won't be much of a guard dog, we thought.

He opened the cage and the puppy came up, crawling on the ground, malnourished and bony with fear in her eyes. She crawled to Bill's shoes, went belly-up and cried. It was a sad sight to see.

"She is the runt of the litter. I can't seem to get her sold," the owner said. "She will need some shots and a checkup. I haven't gotten around to that. I will get rid of her, somehow."

She was six months old, weighed about 28 pounds, and her rib bones protruded. She was mostly black with gold coloring around her eyes and paws. She had big ears that were in the back position, indicating that she was scared.

Still belly-up on Bill's shoe, she started growling at us. Then her parents started growling, barking and showing their teeth. They were large, angry, beautiful dogs, and appeared to want to take a bite if we got close enough.

It was sad to see this small, bony, uncared-for but beautiful pup. We were not prepared to see such a sight, and the odor was so awful you could smell her from a distance. Never having received any vaccinations, she had tapeworms and heartworms, among other medical conditions. She was also dehydrated and hungry. I do not think she had ever had a bath. She was very sick.

The owner talked as if he was going to get rid of her by leaving her in the woods. He was a bit scary himself. We told him that we would come back. We

Heidi

wanted to call our vet to ask for medical advice. We drove off thinking, *She's cute but not in good shape.* When we called our vet, a German Shepherd lover, and told her about the puppy, her words resonated in our hearts: "If you don't rescue her, I will."

The next day we rescued her, and Heidi was ours.

Placing Heidi in a traveling kennel, we drove home with all the car windows down and the AC blowing at full speed to get the smell out of our car.

As soon as we got her home safely in the back yard, she ran under a tree, shaking in fear. It took some time to bathe her, and it took three or four baths to finally get rid of the stench. She had never had a bath. The water scared her and she tried to bite us.

We fixed her a soft and warm bed in a big kennel in our home, which stunk for some time. She cried and growled while staying in the back of her kennel.

Adapting to home

AJ was so excited, bringing Heidi his toys and wanting to play. AJ loved all dogs, so Heidi was welcomed by him on day one. AJ tried every trick to get Heidi to play. He gently pushed toys near her, he nudged her sweetly, he tried to lick her, and would sit near her cage for hours. It seemed like Heidi was perplexed with AJ.

She did not play with his toys or any we bought for her. She growled at AJ, but it did not matter to him. He never gave up.

Having a back yard allowed us to play ball with

her. Having never seen a ball before, it scared her. She tried to bite the first ball we gave her! When it moved, she ran across the yard crying. She feared everyone, and hid behind bushes in the back yard.

The one area where she seemed comfortable was in her kennel. She would sleep in the back of it, despite the door being open. We named her kennel "Heidi's Condo." We left the door open while we were home, so she could come out and play with AJ or us. She stayed in the "condo" most of the time, growling at AJ.

When we fed her, she ate so fast, kernels of food would fly three feet away. She had not had much food in her young life. We came to believe she competed for food with her many brothers and sisters.

Over the months, she was vaccinated and given six months of heartworm treatments, steroids, and other parasitic treatments. She chewed holes in six blankets, a few towels and the heels of my dress shoes; she ate the leather off my slippers and four steps of carpet on our staircase.

Taking care of a puppy is always life changing. She was emotionally unstable being on steroids and heartworm treatments. Being underfed for six months, she was hungry enough, not to mention how the steroids increased her appetite. She tried to eat so many objects that we thought she was going to die of intestinal obstruction instead of heartworms. When she was alone, she would eat the center of a blanket, then tuck it under her so we would not see the damage. I didn't realize what was happening until I began to see maroon and blue flannel in her stool. I found the blankets with holes in them tucked in her "condo."

She eventually began to play with AJ and must have thought of him as her parent. Despite AJ's modeling of kind behavior, Heidi is quite defensive toward most people who come to our house. She will still snap at family and friends. At one point, we thought she would never learn. She still likes to show strangers her bark and teeth.

Heidi out-grew her "condo" and took over the biggest and softest chair in our house. We have not been able to reclaim the chair since. No one gets to sit in that chair without a good ole German Shepherd growl, stare and stalk.

She played with toys occasionally, but for some reason, she hardly played with the store-bought toys we purchased. She did, however, enjoy taking all of AJ's toys and stashing them near her blanket area, but she would not play with them. She growled at AJ if he tried to recover one.

When she would fall asleep, AJ would softly paw his way to her area, take his toy, and go to another space where he would lay on the toy and go to sleep.

In time, Heidi began to get closer to AJ and would sleep next to him most days. When I jogged around the yard with the two of them, AJ would run fast and Heidi would hide behind the trees to attack AJ as he ran by. They would wrestle and have a good time.

Coveted objects

The best toy to Heidi is a cardboard toilet paper roll. She somewhat likes the cardboard roll from paper towels, but not as much. She has an obsession with finding the toilet paper rolls in the trash cans, taking them out quietly, as if we can't see an 80-pound dog walking past us, and hiding them around the house. At first she ate them, but eventually she stopped snacking on cardboard.

She continues to take them from the bathroom trash can, often while we are out of the house, and bring them to her chair, her "toy space." Once she learned not eat them, she began to covet them and would hide them in many places or befriend a guest by placing one at his or her feet. She is masterful at folding a roll down to one-third of its size without eating it. She has hidden them in shoes and slippers and under rugs.

Our family, when sleeping over, finds them under their pillows. It is a special feeling to know that Heidi loves you enough to let you rest your head on a pillow that has a chewed toilet paper cardboard roll underneath it. She sleeps with the cardboard rolls like a child sleeps with a teddy bear. She hides them on beds, in Bill's suitcase when he's packing for a fishing trip, in the cushions of the sofa, under chairs, under Bill's pillow and just about anywhere you can imagine.

After watching her strange behavior, we began

calling her "Heidi Loon." Then we shortened it to "Heidi Lou," to give her a feminine middle name, since she was our first female dog. We also nicknamed her "Enigma Lou."

"Enigma Lou" is a term of endearment to describe this beloved pet that is both strange and sweet simultaneously. Heidi is very smart and crafty. When we leave for church and return an hour or two later, she is likely to be sitting on the same blanket as before we left. Toilet paper rolls, however, are missing. Kleenex are often on the ground and other sundry things are out of place. Her ears are back and belly up. We have come to believe her engimatic behavior is what makes her so charming. The few soft toys she has must be comforting to her in our absence, since when we return home we find that the soft toys have traveled from the toy box to another room.

In addition to her love for toilet paper rolls, she enjoys sitting in the grass and near our gate. She particularly likes to keep watch at the front house window for potential intruders or any people walking, biking, riding or driving down the street.

Truly, no one can enter our property without her notice and subsequent "bark and attack mode." Once off of our property, while certainly capable of attacking, she changes her approach. She is docile and interested in a kinder manner as we walk with her through the neighborhood.

* * * * *

Heidi has blossomed into a sweet and beautiful

dog to people she knows, but if she doesn't know you, beware! Of course, that makes her a great guard dog. Her fur is soft, warm and ever so huggable. She avoids mud, if possible, and perfers not to walk on wet grass.

She does not like to be petted like AJ and Andy did.

Heidi was very sad when AJ died. She seemed lost and without energy for a few months and looked for him. She grieved as much as we did, except we are still grieving AJ, and Heidi has moved into first place quite swiftly.

I taught her leash walking, and once she mastered that she became quite a fun dog to take for daily walks. Over the past few years, she has gotten quite excited about our runs in the nearby neighborhood. Many of the neighbors admire her beautiful coat and accept her strange and sometimes "growly" behavior. Once she knows you and accepts you, you are her friend for life.

Our daily walk has illuminated some additional idiosyncracies of hers. "Freaky Friday" is a term for the day of the week our trash is picked up by the parish trucks. In our neighborhood, the trash cans are set about three feet from the street so the sidewalks and driveways have large blue containers. She does not like the trash cans and walks around them, clearing at least six feet from them. She is extremely sensitive to the sounds the garbage trucks make in picking up cans and backing up with a beep.

Her ears go back, she stops walking and jumps on me to change our direction, avoiding garbage trucks. Once home, she carefully looks out the window to bark when our cans are being emptied.

Friday walks are often cut short or don't happen until the sounds are gone from the neighborhood.

* * * * *

Heidi's rescue and how her personality unfolded have certainly inspired me to write her story. We have met incredible people and learned of foundations that focus on dog rescue, giving me a better understanding of how important the enviexpment is for an animal to grow. The kind and generous people who support these efforts are inspiring to us; they make it safe to adopt rescue dogs and they promote adoptions.

I am grateful that Heidi was not left alone in the woods as a pup to fend for herself. We are so lucky to have her.

Heidi, at this moment, is lying on my feet surrounded by chewed toilet paper cardboard rolls and a partly chewed blanket. She teaches me patience and acceptance.

Chapter 7

Dog loss

This book was a challenge for me to write for several reasons. For one thing, in 2017 AJ died in August and my Father died just two months later.

Losing Dad only four years after Mom died was life-changing for me. Missing them both, I was not interested in writing, especially about death, dying and grief. However, I knew death is a natural part of life — or so I told myself, without much emotion.

I journaled about my sense of loss and prayed for my parents. Journaling became a means of healing for me.

At some point, I began writing this book to speak about pet loss, but soon realized that my dogs helped me with my grief for Mom and Dad and other life transitions. Each of our dogs — Pete Moss, Andy, Buddy, AJ and Heidi — brought joy, love, and unpredictable events to my life.

The loss of each of our dogs has brought sadness and grief as well. The grief from losing a beloved pet is more painful than I ever anticipated. I remember the last day of each dog's life like it was yesterday.

Most grief workshops in which I have participated have focused on human loss. People who can openly discuss pet loss are inspiring to me and are part of my own healing. Honestly, pet loss is not easy to comprehend when one does not know the relationships involved. Exploring this topic further, I wondered how pet loss can be better understood.

The dictionary identifies pet loss categorically under the umbrella of "disenfranchised grief." This is a term that describes grief often not discussed or openly acknowledged by society. Some examples are the death of a friend, death from suicide, loss of a pet, past trauma (sometimes from generations prior), or even the loss of one's home. It is grief that goes unnoticed or unspoken or that is misunderstood. Disenfranchised grief can also be grief experienced from an abortion, miscarriage or infertility; it can be a child's grief due to adoption or the unexpected death of a friend, a parent, or a pet.

Regardless of what it's called, I believe pet loss can be disenfranchised grief, and I recognize my own difficulty in speaking up at times. My own struggle to talk about pet loss continues while I learn how to support others with similar thoughts and feelings. Experiencing the dying and death of Pete Moss, Andy, Buddy and AJ has helped me in learning compassion and understanding for other pet owners.

Truly, no pet is "just a pet." The bonds that develop between pets and people are special.

My hope is that the stories in this book can help

others in recognizing pet loss as part of the journey of pet ownership. There are people who can help us to deal with loss and grief and to move forward with life.

Perhaps you will take the time to write your own pet stories for your children, grandchildren, nieces or nephews. Or just maybe, through this writing, grief and pet loss will be discussed more openly. I hope so.

As God created humans and animals, may He continue to bring us all to a more loving and peaceful world.

My Dogs' Favorite Things

Don't ever let anyone tell you that dogs don't have their own unique personalities. Because they certainly do. Just as no two people are quite alike, the same is true with our furry canine companions.

Our dogs each had their own favorite things to do, or to eat, or to sleep with or play with. These activities ranged from digging up our flower garden or digging out of a fenced-in yard, to chasing rabbits or balls, to "de-stuffing" soft toys. They slept with our t-shirts, or with a stinky blanket, or with a stuffed animal. Look through the next five pages to see the wide variety of our dogs' preferences and peculiarities.

Pete Moss

Best dog friends: Andy, Megan, Lucky the black lab, Sadie and Red

Best human friends: Janice, Boz, Pitts, Sam, Chris D, Alice, Jane, Jeff, Jackie, Jan, Jerry W., Barbara, Cody, Jerry, Doug, Twomey, Francis, Bill and me

Favorite things to do: Licking the can dog food spoon; singing/howling to the piano; napping in the Liriope bed; napping on the staircase; walking with Boz and running with us

Other favorites: Getting bone "Z" treats; chasing rabbits and squirrels; hanging out with family and listening to music

Favorite foods: Tortilla chips, cheese balls, BBQ chicken legs, cheese, ribs, cheese grits, canned dog food, steak on Christmas morning and ice in his water

Favorite sleeping items: Our t-shirts because they smelled like us; a smelly towel; any ball

Favorite toy: Stuffed bear or rabbit

Musical ability: Howl at the moon and sing (howl) when I played the piano

Nickname: Digger Barns

Best Acts: Digging and chasing me naked.

Andy

Best dog friends: Pete Moss, Buddy, Megan of Milton, Lucky, Lizzie, Sadie

Best human friends: Jane, Barbara and Jerry, Steve and Ann, Jeff, Andrew, Jackie, Alex, Zach, Janice, Boz, Pitts, Sylvia, Steve, Bill and me

Favorite things to do: Digging a hole in the mud; burying bones; chewing paper into pieces; walking and running with us or anybody; chasing balls; digging up fruit trees; and sleeping in Liriope monkey grass

Favorite foods: Pete Moss' food, canned dog food, baked chicken

Favorite sleeping item: Stinky blanket

Favorite toy: Any toy he could take from Pete Moss or Buddy

Musical ability: Howl with Pete Moss as I played the piano; rest around the patio listening to Roy Orbison; appreciation for rock 'n' roll

Nicknames: Andrew; Bob Barker; Randy; Anty June (when he ate ants/bugs)

Best Acts: Disappearing for a few days; being sweet.

Buddy

Best dog friends: Andy, AJ and Chessie, Lizzie, Lexi

Best human friends: Jane, Barbara and Jerry, Steve and Ann, Cody, Ali, Janice, Jeff and Jackie, Alex, Jan and Jerry, Steve and Sylvia, Mom (with a towel on her lap), and Francis, Bill and me

Favorite things to do: Play ball, chase AJ, run for balls, catch balls thrown on the roof and bouncing down, pop up balls by rolling them under his paw, de-stuffing soft toys

Favorite foods: Meatballs, yogurt, canned dog food

Favorite sleeping item: Ball

Favorite toy: Ball and the stuffed jack toy; rubber bone with noise-maker inside

Musical ability: Squeeze toy

Nicknames: Dupont, Bud Zee, Jurassic Dog and Ball Dog

Best Act: rolling the ball with his paw to pop up in the air and catching it in his mouth.

A J

Best dog friends: Buddy, Heidi, Emmie, Lexi, Lizzie Twig and Abby

Best human friends: Anyone who came to our house: Lizzy, Barbara, Jerry, Jeff, Jan and Jerry, Sue, Francis and Cathi, Andrew, Edith, Cody, Ali, Corey, Sylvia, Steve, Anne, Janice. Also, Bill and me, of course.

Favorite things to do: Run, run for balls, de-stuffing soft toys, play tug of war with a towel, play anything, chase and be chased.

Favorite foods: Canned dog food, bones, steak.

Favorite sleeping items: Stuffed animals and Mom's Ragin' Cajun blanket

Favorite toys: Samuel, a used lavender de-stuffed rabbit; de-stuffed jack toy; stuffed gold lion toy

Musical ability: Barking

Nicknames: Pillow with a heartbeat, Anty, Cute Zee, Anty June 2, Mustards, AKA Lege, Ajanee (ah jun-nay), Velcro, *Ajanee La Bois Fontaine*, Water Dog

Best acts: Un-latching gates, de-stuffing toys.

Heidi

Best dog friends: AJ, Trigger and Emmie

Best human friends: Jackie, Barbara, Jeff, Jan and Jerry, Francis and Cathi, Bob, Edith, Ellen, Corey, Ali, Bill and me

Favorite things to do: Bark and hide cardboard toilet paper rolls around the house; run Zee

Favorite foods: Canned dog food, yogurt, milk bones and chicken

Favorite sleeping items: Cardboard toilet paper roll, tomato blanket, and any chewed blanket

Favorite toy: Cardboard toilet paper roll

Musical ability: Sleeping under my piano

Nicknames: Heidi Loon, Lou, Enigma Lou; Heidi Lou, Miss Lou and Me-Jae

Best acts: Stalking cardboard toilet paper rolls in the trash and taking them when we were away.

Appendix 2

The Rainbow Bridge

Just this side of heaven is a place called Rainbow Bridge.

When an animal dies that has been especially close to someone here, that pet goes to Rainbow Bridge. There are meadows and hills for all of our special friends so they can run and play together. There is plenty of food, water, and sunshine, and our friends are warm and comfortable.

All the animals who had been ill and old are restored to health and vigor. Those who were hurt or maimed are made whole and strong again, just as we remember them in our dreams of days and times gone by. The animals are happy and content, except for one small thing; they each miss someone very special to them, who had to be left behind.

They all run and play together, but the day comes when one suddenly stops and looks into the distance. His bright eyes are intent. His eager body quivers. Suddenly he begins to run from the group, flying over the green grass, his legs carrying him faster and faster.

You have been spotted, and when you and your special friend finally meet, you cling together in joyous reunion, never to be parted again. The happy kisses rain upon your face; your hands again caress the beloved head, and you look once more into the trusting eyes of your pet, so long gone from your life but never absent from your heart.

Then you cross Rainbow Bridge together.

(Author Unknown)

Appendix 3

The Blessing Cup

Every family strives to strengthen its bonds by mutually sharing hopes and fears, joys and sorrows.

The Blessing Cup is a family tradition you can begin in your home to help you toward this goal. It is a sign of solidarity, of oneness in prayer and purpose.

The Blessing Cup service is centered around a common cup and based on the use of Scripture and petition. The cup is made of metal, pottery or glass and should be filled with a beverage that fits the occasion and the taste of the participants. All in attendance should drink from the cup. It is kept in a prominent place in the home as a reminder of the family's mutual hope.

It is used as the family gathers for prayer at special times – holidays, birthdays, anniversaries; times of change, growth and loss.

Among the many family traditions noted in the book, *The Blessing Cup*, is the Funeral Service for a Pet, presented on the facing page. ▶

Funeral Service For A Pet
(In the Christian Tradition)

From the book, *The Blessing Cup*,
by Rock Travnikar, OFM (Franciscan priest)

Opening Prayer

> Master and Lord of all creation, hear the prayer we offer you in the name of the Father, and of the Son, and of the Holy Spirit.

Scripture

> Are not five sparrows sold for two pennies? Yet not one of them is forgotten in God's sight. (Luke 12:6)

Petitions

> You have shown us affection and faithfulness through all of creation. We are grateful as we pray.
>
> *Response:* Comfort us, Lord.
>
> We remember the laughter and joy which _____ has given us, and we pray.
>
> Help us to share kindness and care with all living things, we pray.
>
> *Add your own petitions.*

Collect

> In your goodness you have called us to be stewards of all creation. We take up this cup, grateful for having been entrusted with the care of this creature. We marvel at how you have fashioned and formed our world in harmony and peace.

Sharing of the Blessing Cup

> Pray together the Our Father.

Acknowledgements

I dedicate this book to my dear husband, Bill, who taught me nearly everything I know about our dogs; he is truly a dog's best friend.

I acknowledge with much gratitude Monique Burdin and Fr. Louis Richard, who inspired me to write this book and to tell the stories of the dogs in my life.

A great big "thank you" also to my sister-in-law Cathi Pavy, Sr. Carm Latiolais, and Sylvia Oats for their support along the way as I worked through these stories, sometimes tearfully but more often joyfully and with gratitude for the time I had with my beloved pets.

About the Author...

CAMILLE PAVY CLAIBOURNE, APRN, PhD, is a pet lover and nationally recognized expert in nursing. As a Registered Nurse of 40-plus years, she is always looking for opportunities to help others in need. She is actively involved in her community through the University of Louisiana at Lafayette, as a volunteer for Hospice of Acadiana, and through St. Joseph Catholic Church of Milton, La. Her work in thanatology, the study of death and dying, has been her main professional focus since 2001.

She has authored four books: *Pathways to Hope* (1996); *Dying in God's Hands* (2007); *Purses and Shoes for Sale: The joys and challenges of caring for elderly parents* (2016); and *Dog Love & Dog Loss* (2021). For more information, visit www.acadianhouse.com.

Books by
Camille Pavy Claibourne

Dog Love & Dog Loss

A-100 page softcover book in which the author happily recounts her experiences with the dogs she has loved and shared her home with for most of her adult life. A nationally recognized expert in thanatology (the study of death and dying), the author also explores the delicate subject of losing a beloved pet and offers understanding and support for grieving pet owners. The book includes appendices: "Funeral Services for a Pet" and "The Rainbow Bridge," a poem about the joyful reunion with our pets in the afterlife. (Author: Camille Pavy Claibourne. ISBN: 1-7352641-9-9. Price $11.95.)

Dying In God's Hands

A 152-page hardcover book that provides keen insights into the hearts and minds of the dying. It is based on a dozen or more interviews with terminally ill hospice patients, in which they share their hopes, dreams, fears and needs. The majority of the interviews provide evidence that faith in God and belief in the hereafter are the greatest strengths of the dying. Designed to comfort the dying and their loved ones, the book also contains a section of prayers and prose from all major world religions. (Author: Camille Pavy Claibourne. ISBN: 0-925417-64-5. Price: $16.95)

Purses & Shoes For Sale
The Joys and Challenges of Caring for Elderly Parents

A 216-page hardcover book about the author's journey as a caregiver to her elderly parents in the twilight of their lives. Packed with suggestions on how to deal with issues encountered by adult children of the elderly. Includes a Q&A section with answers to frequently asked questions, plus a resources section with practical advice, useful websites and a glossary of terms. (Author: Camille Pavy Claibourne. Hardcover ISBN: 0-925417-96-3. Price: $17.95. Softcover ISBN: 0-925417-49-1. Price $14.95)

TO ORDER, list the books you wish to purchase along with the corresponding cost of each. For shipping in the U.S., add $4 for the first book, and $1 per book thereafter. Louisiana residents add 9% tax to the cost of the books. Mail your order and check or credit card authorization (VISA/MC/AmEx) to: Acadian House Publishing, P.O. Box 52247, Lafayette, LA 70505. Or call (800) 850-8851. To order online, go to www.acadianhouse.com.